Vim and Vig Go by Canoe

By Carmel Reilly

Vim and Vig had lots of food.

Vim had some bamboo shoots.

Vig had some sweet blooms.

Vim looked in the pool.

Vim put her bamboo shoots
in the shoe.

She put Vig's blooms in, too.

They slid the shoe canoe into the pool and got in.

At first, the canoe did not go the right way.

We can not steer our shoe canoe!

I told you a shoe is not a canoe, Vim!

Vim got the canoe going
the right way.

But soon it started to sink!

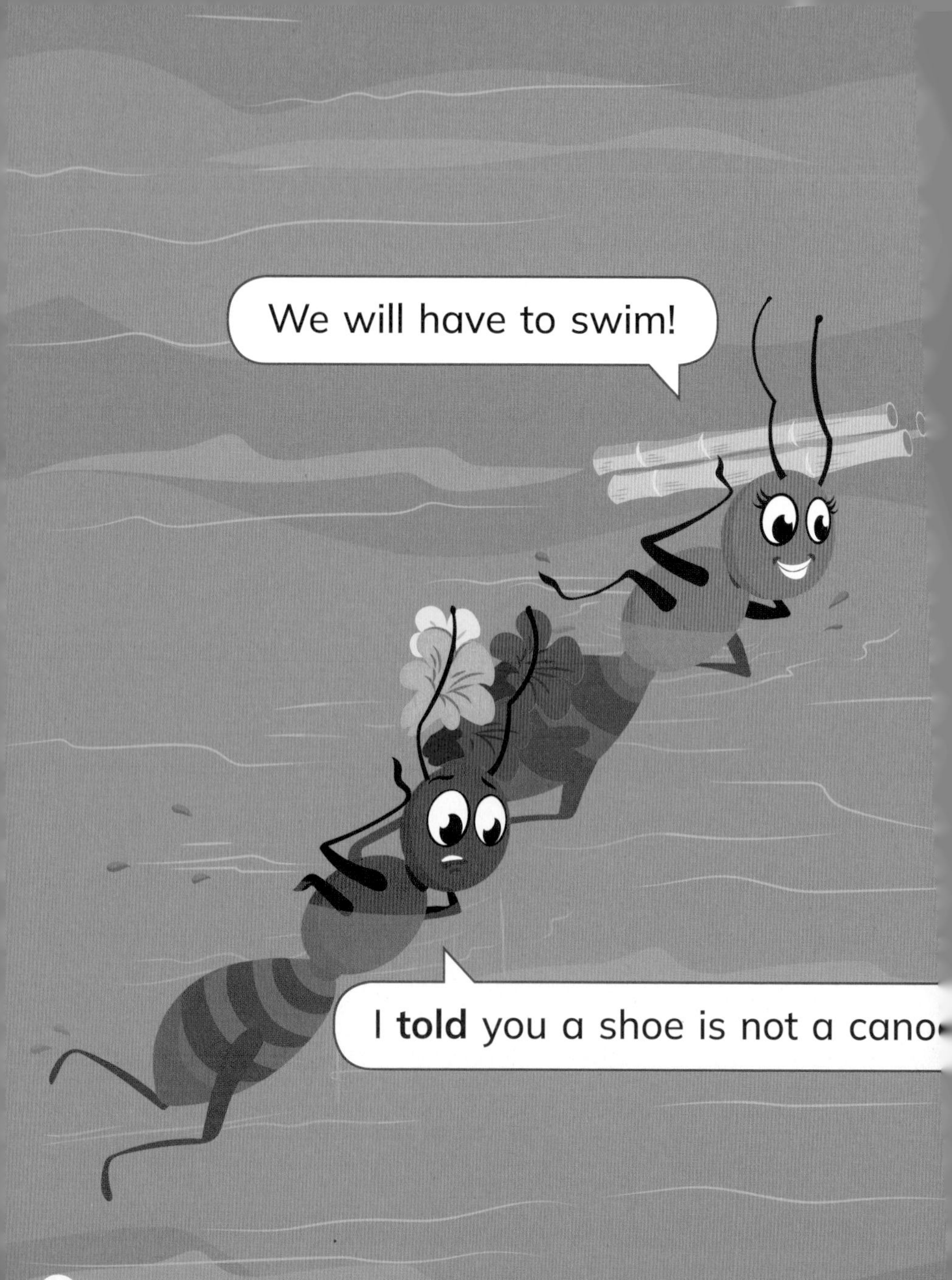
We will have to swim!
I **told** you a shoe is not a cano

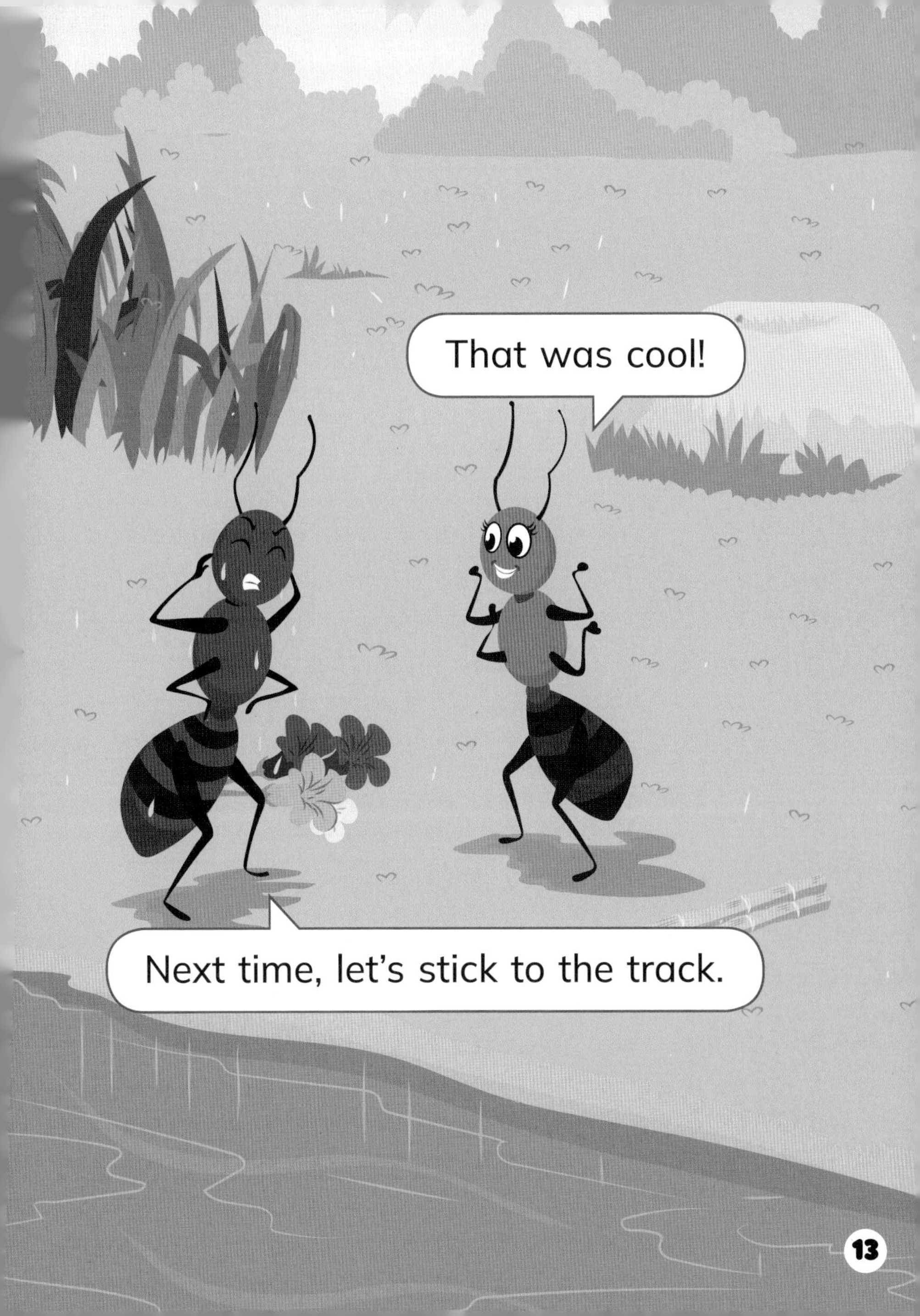
That was cool!
Next time, let's stick to the track.

CHECKING FOR MEANING

1. What food had Vig and Vim collected? *(Literal)*

2. Where did Vim find the shoe? *(Literal)*

3. Why do you think the shoe canoe started to sink? *(Inferential)*

EXTENDING VOCABULARY

bamboo	What is *bamboo*? How does it grow? What is it used for?
blooms	Tell students that *blooms* are the flowers of a plant. What might Vig do with the blooms when he gets home?
canoe	What is a *canoe*? (A small, narrow boat.) Tell students that the word *canoe* has two syllables, with the long /oo/ sound appearing in the second syllable.

MOVING BEYOND THE TEXT

1. Have you ever been in a boat? Have you paddled a canoe? What did you use and what did you have to do? How do you steer a canoe?

2. What are some other types of boats you know? How are they similar and different? E.g. kayak, liner, trawler, speedboat.

3. Talk about why Vim wanted to go across the pool instead of taking the track. Which way would have been quicker and why?

4. Can you think of other ways Vim and Vig could have gone across the pool? What could they have used to help them?

SPEED SOUNDS

oo	ue	ew	ui	u_e

ou	u	oe	o

PRACTICE WORDS

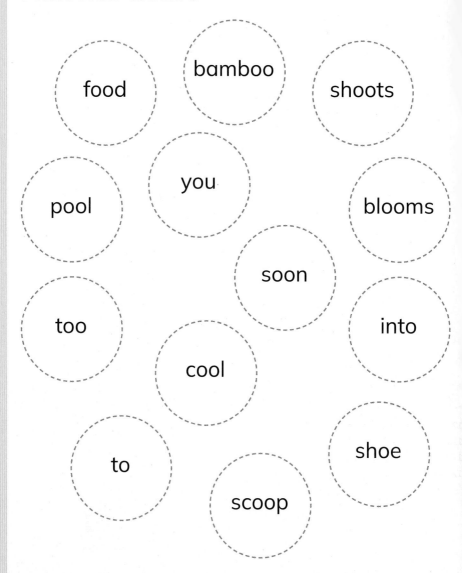

food

bamboo

shoots

pool

you

blooms

soon

too

into

cool

to

shoe

scoop